CW00408139

LESSONS ON LIVING FROM
SOLOMON

A devotional by
WOODROW KROLL

BACK TO THE BIBLE
Publishing

SOLOMON
published by Back to the Bible Publishing
©1998 by Woodrow Kroll

International Standard Book Number
0-8474-0691-1

Edited by Rachel Derowitsch
Cover design by Robert Greuter
& Associates

For information:
BACK TO THE BIBLE
POST OFFICE BOX 82808
LINCOLN, NEBRASKA 68501

1 2 3 4 5 6 7 8—04 03 02 01 00 99 98

Printed in the USA

CONTENTS

DAY 1

Now Adonijah the son of Haggith exalted himself, saying, "I will be king"; and he prepared for himself chariots and horsemen, and fifty men to run before him.

The Would-Be King

Self-centeredness keeps us from truly caring about others. One of the saddest characters in American literature is Willy Loman in Arthur Miller's classic play *Death of a Salesman*. Poor Willy. He was always going to make that "big sale." He was going to bring home a fortune one day—then people would give him the recognition that he truly deserved. But the big sale never came. Willy even boasted of the number of people who would come to his funeral, for everybody loves a salesman. But the only people who attended Willy's funeral were his wife and two sons, the ones whom he neglected most while he played the big shot.

Adonijah was afflicted with the same problem. His father, King David, was old and feeble but had not yet publicly appointed an heir. Instead of considering his father's wishes, Adonijah decided he would "exalt himself." He was a self-appointed king. Furthermore, his actions reflected the attitude that he considered his father as good as dead. He never saw beyond himself.

American culture encourages self-centeredness. Slogans such as "You deserve a break today," "Grab all the gusto" and "Have it your way" can seduce even Christians into believing that life revolves around their own whims and wishes. How different this attitude is from what the New Testament teaches. We are commanded to "love one another" (John 13:34), "receive one another" (Rom. 15:7), "serve one another" (Gal. 5:13) and "forgive one another" (Col. 3:13). Instead of exalting ourselves, Scripture exhorts us to be concerned about the welfare of others.

Be careful not to buy into the "me-first" philosophy that permeates our world today. Ask God to give you a heart that is sensitive to the needs of others. Pray for others. Demonstrate your concern for others in the way you care for their needs. And trust God to provide for you as He provides for others through you. It's the way to beat the trap of self-centeredness.

Exalt others and let God exalt you.

Reflections/Prayer Requests

_____

_____

_____

_____

_____

DAY 2

1 Kings 1:7

Then he conferred with Joab the son of Zeruiah and with Abiathar the priest, and they followed and helped Adonijah.

Friends Who Fail

Aristotle claimed that a friend in "one soul dwelling in two bodies." Others have defined a friend as "a person who knows all about us and still likes us." Newspaper columnist Walter Winchell suggested that a friend is one "who walks in when others walk out." However you define a friendship, it is obvious that when a friend fails us, the pain can be devastating.

In his latter days, David experienced the failure of not just one friend but two. One was Joab, David's nephew and the commander of his armies; the other was Abiathar, the high priest. Both of them sided with Adonijah, David's son and brother of Absalom, when he decided to exalt himself as king. These men had served faithfully with David. Abiathar had been with him as far back as the days when David first fled from Saul (1 Sam. 22:20). And Joab had been the genius behind much of David's success as king. The pain of their treachery must have been excruciating for the aging and ailing king.

How often, even among Christians, do friends fail us. Sometimes they deliberately turn their backs on us; other times they simply vanish from our lives due to unforeseen circumstances such as moving away, sickness or death. Ultimately, all of our friends fail us in some way and we feel hurt. We must know, however, that there is a friend who never fails. The Book of Proverbs says, "There is a friend who sticks closer than a brother" (18:24). That friend is Jesus. He promised us, "I am with you always, even to the end of the age" (Matt. 28:20).

Are you experiencing the pain of a failed friendship? Has your best friend moved away and left you friendless? Or worse, has someone turned against you and you feel betrayed? Then turn to Jesus. He will understand (His friends did the same to Him), and He will stand by you whatever your circumstances. Jesus is a friend who never fails.

When all other friends fail you, your friend Jesus is faithful.

Reflections/Prayer Requests

_____

_____

_____

_____

_____

_____

DAY 3

I Kings 1:33

The king also said to them, "Take with you the servants of your lord, and have Solomon my son ride on my own mule, and take him down to Gihon."

A Gentle Spirit

Richard Weaver earned his living in the mines, but his higher priority was bringing others to Christ. One day a fellow said to Weaver, "I'm sick of your constant preaching. I've a good mind to smack you in the face!" "Go ahead if it will make you feel better," Weaver replied. The man struck him. The Christian did not retaliate but turned the other cheek. Again the unbeliever hit him and then walked away. Weaver called after him, "I forgive you and still pray that the Lord will save you!" The next morning his assailant was waiting for him. He asked, "Dick, do you really forgive me?" "Certainly," Weaver said, and again shared the message of salvation. God opened the man's heart, and he received Christ as his Savior. Gentleness and humility had won the day.

As Solomon prepared to take his place as king, he rode on the back of a lowly mule, not an impressive warhorse. His reign was not to be marked by power and brute force but by wisdom exercised in gentleness and humility. While his father,

David, achieved great honor through warfare, Solomon far excelled him (1 Kings 3:13) without having to resort to the same tactics.

When we are faced with opposition, it is tempting to overpower it by sheer strength. If someone dares to stand in our way, we run over him. Yet this is not normally God's way. What we accomplish in a spirit of gentleness, as we seek peace and reconciliation, will outlast what we achieve by the "bulldozer approach." And it leaves a better testimony as well.

If you're facing opposition from someone at work, at home or in church, ask God to give you a gentle spirit. Seek His wisdom to deal with the conflict humbly. Put aside any pride that might be a stumbling block to your success, and determine with God's help to respond with meekness. The effects will be more satisfying and more permanent.

Brute force is only for brutes.

Reflections/Prayer Requests

_____

_____

_____

_____

_____

_____

DAY 4

1 Kings 1:40

And all the people went up after him; and the people played the flutes and rejoiced with great joy, so that the earth seemed to split with their sound.

The Joy of the Lord

A middle-aged schoolteacher invested her life savings in a business enterprise that turned out to be a swindle. When her investment disappeared and the wonderful dream was shattered, she went to the local office of the Better Business Bureau. "Why on earth didn't you come to us first?" they asked. "Didn't you know about the Better Business Bureau?" "Oh, yes," the teacher said sadly, "I've always known about you. But I didn't come because I was afraid you'd tell me not to do it."

That's the attitude many people have toward God. They know that He's there, but they're afraid to come to Him because He might throw a wet blanket on their plans. They know He'll tell them the truth; they just don't want to hear it.

When Solomon, God's choice for Israel's king, proceeded to be crowned, the hearts of the people were filled with joy. The procession down to Gihon, where Solomon was officially declared king, was filled with the sound of music and celebration. This is the way it should be with us too. Obeying the will of the Lord is always a cause for rejoicing, not a cause for mourning.

Satan would have us believe that God is a killjoy. He lies to us and tells us that the farther we stay away from what God wants, the greater our chances to be truly happy. But countless people have been ruined by Satan's lies. Only the Lord is able to give true, lasting joy. The closer we walk with Him, the more cause we have to rejoice.

Discover for yourself what a joy it is to walk in God's will. You will learn that there is a direct relationship between obedience to God and joy from God. Let the joy of the Lord fill your heart. Ask Him to remove anything that is preventing you from fully experiencing His joy. Then discover the delight of obeying Jesus.

Joy is inextricably tied to Jesus.

Reflections/Prayer Requests

_____
_____
_____
_____
_____
_____
_____
_____

DAY 5

1 Kings 2:2–3

"I go the way of all the earth; be strong, therefore, and prove yourself a man. And keep the charge of the LORD your God: to walk in His ways, to keep His statutes, His commandments, His judgments, and His testimonies, as it is written in the Law of Moses, that you may prosper in all that you do and wherever you turn."

The Key to Prosperity

Many young people fantasize about the possibility of becoming a sports star. And little wonder. According to one source, Michael Jordan earns more than $300,000 a game (that's $10,000 a minute, assuming he averages 30 minutes per game). In December 1998, the Los Angeles Dodgers signed pitcher Kevin Brown to a $105-million contract. With those kinds of dollars being spent on athletes, prosperity for them seems like a sure thing.

Yet the true secret to affluence doesn't lie in landing a lucrative sports contract. Solomon's father, David, knew that real prosperity comes from being obedient to the Lord. Unlike those who seek only the benefit of financial gain, David assured Solomon that obeying God would result in prosperity in "all that you do and wherever you turn."

Although we may legitimately question whether any athlete is worth the kind of money mentioned, there is certainly nothing wrong with material abundance. But we must recognize that it counts for little when compared to spiritual prosperity and the well-being of those we love. Mere dollars and cents cannot turn back the hands of time or restore the ravages of loose living. It is especially in these important areas of life that living according to God's Word pays the greatest dividends.

Don't be lulled into thinking that prosperity is based on a bank account. Jesus said, "For what will it profit a man if he gains the whole world, and loses his own soul?" (Mark 8:36). Where do you find your prosperity? Is it in the temporal, the financial, the pleasurable? Make sure your prosperity is built on your walk with God rather than on your wealth in this world.

The key to real prosperity is found in God, not in gold.

Reflections/Prayer Requests

_____

_____

_____

_____

_____

DAY 6

1 Kings 3:1

Now Solomon made a treaty with Pharaoh king of Egypt, and married Pharaoh's daughter; then he brought her to the City of David until he had finished building his own house, and the house of the LORD, and the wall all around Jerusalem.

Unequally Yoked

We often receive letters at Back to the Bible from heartbroken parents whose children were raised as Christians but have chosen to marry unbelievers. We also get letters from Christians who married outside the faith and now are experiencing the heartaches that such unions bring. In the long run, marriage to an unbeliever invariably brings grief.

No one discovered that more tragically than did Solomon. In his early years as Israel's king, he made a treaty with Pharaoh, king of Egypt. The custom of that day was to seal such a relationship by marriage. This was not a union of two people who loved each other; it was a business deal. But such an arrangement made Solomon responsible to see that all the needs of his Egyptian wife were met, including her religious needs. As time passed, Solomon made more treaties and collected more wives with various religious backgrounds. In the end, 1 Kings

11:3 tells us he had 700 wives (not to mention 300 concubines) and "his wives turned away his heart."

The Bible warns us not to be intimately involved with unbelievers. Paul calls it being "unequally yoked" (2 Cor. 6:14). This involves not only marriage but also business partnerships and other relationships where moral and ethical issues are at stake. Such alliances will entangle us with the values of the world (2 Tim. 2:4) and seriously compromise our walk with the Lord.

If you are contemplating becoming involved intimately with an unbeliever, heed God's warning. Save yourself and others from a great deal of heartache. Don't bind yourself to someone to whom you cannot bind yourself spiritually. If you are already involved, ask God to protect you from harming your relationship with Him. Pray earnestly for the unbeliever in your life and set a godly example for him or her.

If you can't pull together, don't get together.

Reflections/Prayer Requests

_____

_____

_____

_____

DAY 7

1 Kings 3:8–9

*"And Your servant is in the midst of Your peo-
ple whom You have chosen, a great people,
too numerous to be numbered or counted.
Therefore give to Your servant an understanding heart to judge Your people, that I may dis-
cern between good and evil. For who is able
to judge this great people of Yours?"*

An Understanding Heart

A lack of understanding can cause a
great deal of embarrassment. President
Coolidge once invited some friends from
Vermont to dine at the White House. They
were worried about their table manners,
so they decided to do everything their host
did. All went well until coffee was served.
Coolidge poured part of his into the
saucer. The guests did the same. The president then added sugar and cream. So did
the visitors. Finally Coolidge leaned over
and placed his saucer on the floor for the
cat!

King Solomon was faced with something more serious than a simple faux pas.
He would be responsible for the lives of
millions of people. His decisions would
create a ripple effect that would reach well
beyond the borders of his own land. His
wisdom, or lack of it, would bring either
prosperity or ruin to the entire nation.
Therefore, it is understandable why he felt

16

an overwhelming need for a heart that could correctly assess a situation and distinguish between good and evil.

This need is still very real for you and me today. Even though we may not wield quite the influence of Solomon, the decisions we make certainly affect our family, our work and, through exercising the privilege of voting, our community, state and nation. When pooled with other believers, we influence far more than our family; we can change our country. That makes it imperative for us to seek an understanding heart from God as well.

The Book of Proverbs urges, "And in all your getting, get understanding" (4:7). Ask God to give you an understanding heart, especially when it comes to decisions that affect your family, your church and your country. Acknowledge your inability to always distinguish good from evil, and seek God's discernment instead.

Discernment begins with God.

Reflections/Prayer Requests

_____

_____

_____

_____

_____

_____

DAY 8

1 Kings 3:12–13

"Behold, I have done according to your words; see, I have given you a wise and understanding heart, so that there has not been anyone like you before you, nor shall any like you arise after you. And I have also given you what you have not asked: both riches and honor, so that there shall not be anyone like you among the kings all your days."

Superabundant Blessings

Howard Hendricks, professor emeritus at Dallas Theological Seminary, told a story about a couple in Christian ministry who had four children. While things were financially rough, Timmy, the youngest, asked, "Dad, do you think Jesus would mind if I asked for a shirt?" "Well, of course not," his father replied. So every day they prayed for a shirt. Several weeks later the mother received a call from a merchant who inquired, "Could you use some boys' shirts?" "How many do you have?" she asked hesitantly. He said, "Twelve." That night when Timmy began to pray for a shirt, his father said, "We don't have to pray for the shirt, Timmy. The Lord has answered your prayer." Older brother Tom went out of the room and brought back one shirt. Then he went out again and brought back another, and another—until he had piled 12 shirts on the table. Timmy thought God had gone into the shirt business! Today, there is another young boy who believes that God is able to provide superabundantly.

Solomon also discovered that God is no miser. Instead of just the wisdom and understanding the newly crowned king asked for, God gave him riches and honor in abundance as well. Solomon became known as both the wealthiest and wisest king of his time. He found that God's blessings were not simply sufficient; they were overflowing.

Are you expecting God to provide for your needs? Do you think He will give you only the bare necessities? Don't cheat yourself. Expect a lot more from God. He blesses superabundantly. While it isn't always in the material realm, God never fails to give His children blessings in profusion. Our God is the God of abundance. Let Him bless you abundantly.

God's blessings are never just the minimum daily requirement.

Reflections/Prayer Requests

_____

_____

_____

_____

_____

DAY 9

1 Kings 3:23–25

And the king said, "The one says, 'This is my son, who lives, and your son is the dead one'; and the other says, 'No! But your son is the dead one, and my son is the living one.'" Then the king said, "Bring me a sword." So they brought a sword before the king. And the king said, "Divide the living child in two, and give half to one, and half to the other."

Know-how Plus

How many times have you come across a new invention and thought, *I could have invented that!* Recently I walked though an area at work where employees at Back to the Bible are allowed to display items for sale. Someone had come up with a nifty wooden rack for displaying Beanie Babies. Anyone could have invented it, yet it took someone who not only thought of the idea but actually made the product to reap the benefits. Wisdom is knowing the right thing to do and then doing it at the right time.

Solomon demonstrated that kind of practical wisdom. Faced with the need to determine the true mother of a newborn, he resorted to what he knew about motherhood. He applied that knowledge by suggesting the child be cut in two, with half given to each woman who claimed to be the child's mother. As expected, the real mother refused while the false claimant was willing to go along with the suggestion. The writer of 1 Kings says the people heard of this judgment and "feared the king, for they saw that the wisdom of God was in him to administer justice" (3:28).

Knowledge is important in a Christian's life (2 Pet. 1:5), but we also need the wisdom to apply it. It's not sufficient to have the know-how—we have to do something with that know-how. Only as God shows us how to apply what we know can we lay claim to the gift of wisdom.

Are you lacking in wisdom? James says, "Ask of God" (James 1:5). Ask God to give you not only knowledge but also the practical wisdom of knowing how to apply it.

Wisdom puts feet to your knowledge.

Reflections/Prayer Requests

_____

_____

_____

_____

_____

_____

_____

DAY 10

1 Kings 5:6

"Now therefore, command that they [the servants of Hiram] cut down cedars for me from Lebanon; and my servants will be with your servants, and I will pay you wages for your servants according to whatever you say. For you know there is none among us who has skill to cut timber like the Sidonians."

Teamwork

Don Bennett, a Seattle businessman, decided he wanted to climb Washington's Mount Rainier. It's a stiff climb to the peak of the 14,410-foot summit, but so many individuals have succeeded that it no longer merits much attention. But for Bennett, the climb was a remarkable achievement. He made the climb on one leg and two crutches. Asked to share the most important lesson he learned, Bennett gave credit to the team of individuals who helped him attain his dream. He observed, "You can't do it alone."

Solomon realized this same truth. When he became king, he inherited from his father not only the kingdom but also the task of building a temple worthy of the God of the universe. Such an awesome responsibility would have been overwhelming, but Solomon knew it could be done if he called on others to help. Accordingly, he contacted a friend of his father, King

Hiram of Tyre, and requested his most skilled lumbermen. The king graciously agreed. And thanks to the benefit of teamwork, they built one of the most beautiful temples ever.

Christians are notorious for not working together as a team. Some try to worship God on their own. The writer of Hebrews had to admonish such people about "forsaking the assembling of ourselves together" (10:25). Others can be difficult to get along with (1 Cor. 1:11). But whatever we accomplish alone is not nearly what we could have accomplished with others.

Are you willing to be a team player? Can your pastor count on you to pitch in with others in your church when there is a job to be done? More will get done if we do it together. Learn from the wisdom of Solomon. Be a part of something greater than yourself. Be a part of a team.

The best work is teamwork.

Reflections/Prayer Requests

_____

_____

_____

_____

_____

_____

DAY 11

1 Kings 6:12–13

*"Concerning this temple which you are build-
ing, if you walk in My statutes, execute My
judgments, keep all My commandments, and
walk in them, then I will perform My word with
you, which I spoke to your father David. And I
will dwell among the children of Israel, and
will not forsake My people Israel."*

The Comforter

In 1858 Scottish missionary John G.
Paton and his wife sailed for the New He-
brides. Three months after arriving on the
island of Tanna, his wife died in childbirth.
One week later his infant son also died.
Paton was plunged into sorrow. Sur-
rounded by savage people, he wrote, "Let
those who have ever passed through any
similar darkness as of midnight feel for
me. As for all others, it would be more
than vain to try to paint my sorrows. But
for Jesus, and [His] fellowship—I [would]
have gone mad and died."

God knew that Israel would need this
kind of comfort too. After the reign of
Solomon, the nation would divide between north and south. Over the next several hundred years various armies would
occupy the land and bring havoc upon the
people. God's solution? He promised, "I
will dwell among the children of Israel,
and will not forsake My people Israel"

(1 Kings 6:13). God's presence, as represented by His temple, would be their ultimate comfort.

Believers today don't have a temple made of wood and stone; they have something even better. They have the presence of God in the person of the Holy Spirit dwelling in them. Jesus promised, "And I will pray the Father, and He will give you another Helper" (John 14:16). When we received Christ as our Savior, our bodies became the home of the One who is called Comforter (John 14:26; 15:26; 16:7, KJV).

If you lack this kind of comfort and courage, first make sure that you have received Jesus Christ as your Savior. If you are saved, then see if there is any sin hindering the Holy Spirit's work in you. In the midst of difficulties and disasters, He is there to encourage you to go on despite your circumstances.

He who dwells in us
also goes with us.

Reflections/Prayer Requests

_____

_____

_____

_____

_____

DAY 12

1 Kings 8:5

Also King Solomon, and all the congregation of Israel who were assembled with him, were with him before the ark, sacrificing sheep and oxen that could not be counted or numbered for multitude.

No Sacrifice Too Great

Japanese folklore tells of a rice farmer whose land overlooked the village where his friends lived. While working in his rice paddies one day, he felt a quake and saw the distant ocean swiftly withdraw from the shoreline. He knew there would soon be a devastating tidal wave. In the valley below, he saw his neighbors working fields that soon would be flooded. They would have to run to his hilltop or die. His rice barns were dry as tinder. To get the people quickly to higher ground, the farmer set fire to his barns and then rang the fire gong. His neighbors saw the smoke and rushed up the hill to help him. When they looked back from their place of safety, they saw the tidal wave wash over the fields they had just left. Instantly they understood. The farmer had made a great sacrifice that they might be saved.

Solomon and the people of Israel were equally generous in their sacrifices. They were so enthused about the new temple and the blessings that God was giving them that no sacrifice was withheld. They brought so many sheep and oxen for offerings that they couldn't be counted. They loved God so much that no sacrifice was too great.

Jesus felt the same way about you and me. Being crucified was a terrible way to die; to be separated from His Father was even worse (Matt. 27:46). Yet He loved us so much that no sacrifice was too great. The writer of Hebrews says that Jesus endured the cross for "the joy that was set before Him" (12:2). Our salvation made it all worthwhile.

Knowing how Jesus Christ feels about you, how does that make you feel about Him? Since no sacrifice was too great for Him to make for you, what should your response be? Is there any sacrifice too great to make for Him? Jesus gave His all. What do you have that you need to give to Him today?

Jesus' all demands our all.

Reflections/Prayer Requests

_____

_____

_____

_____

_____

_____

DAY 13

I Kings 8:10–11

And it came to pass, when the priests came out of the holy place, that the cloud filled the house of the LORD, so that the priests could not continue ministering because of the cloud; for the glory of the LORD filled the house of the LORD.

Be Filled

There are many occasions in life where it's essential that some things be absolutely full. If you're headed out for a long trip, for example, the gas tank needs to be filled. A half of a tank just won't do. Or when the doctor writes a prescription for antibiotics for you, he always tells you to take all the pills, even after you feel better. Take the full dose; a partial dose won't insure that you'll get better.

When Solomon and the people of Israel dedicated the temple, it was important for God to make His presence known in complete fullness. It was God's way of putting His stamp of approval both on Solomon and on the structure he built for the Lord's glory. An anemic demonstration of God's presence would not be sufficient. So God chose to fill the temple with the cloud of His glory until the priests had to halt temporarily the offering of sacrifices. His presence was so overwhelming that those who served Him had to vacate the premises.

A Christian needs to experience this same filling as well. The Lord's glory (or character) needs to so fill our lives that we overflow with God's goodness, purity and all the other traits that make up who He is. That's why the apostle Paul wrote, "And do not be drunk with wine, in which is dissipation; but be filled with the Spirit" (Eph. 5:18). Not just once, as when the temple was dedicated, but continually be filled. And not just a little bit, but be filled all the way, right to the brim, until the Spirit of God spills out from you.

Ask God to fill you with His glory through the Holy Spirit (Luke 11:13). Don't be satisfied with a nominal, lukewarm Christianity. Pray that God's character will so fill you that it will flow out to everyone around you.

He who is full of God can never be full of himself.

Reflections/Prayer Requests

_____

_____

_____

_____

_____

_____

_____

_____

DAY 14

1 Kings 8:27

"But will God indeed dwell on the earth? Behold, heaven and the heaven of heavens cannot contain You. How much less this temple which I have built!"

How Big Is God?

Years ago when the city fathers of New York contemplated the future growth of their city, they plotted the streets and numbered them from the center outward. At the time, New York consisted of only six or seven streets. In their planning maps, they projected how large they thought the city might grow. Reaching beyond their wildest imagination, they drew streets on the map all the way out to a 19th street. They called it "Boundary Street" because they were sure that was as large as New York City would become. But history proved them to be shortsighted. At last count, the metropolis had reached beyond 284th Street.

Solomon labored under no such delusions when it came to God. He had built the largest man-made structure in Israel. (Interior dimensions of the temple were at least 90 feet long, 30 feet wide and 45 feet high, according to 1 Kings 6:2.) Yet this builder-king knew that even the heaven of heavens was unable to contain God, not to mention a building. God was far larger than anything Solomon could build.

In our desire to be intimate with God, we often try to shrink Him down to a size we're comfortable with. If God were too big, so our thinking goes, His awesomeness would threaten to overwhelm us. Therefore, we are prone to think of God in the small, cuddly size—someone little enough to fit in our back pocket. Yet in doing so, we miss the comfort of knowing a God who is greater than any challenge life may set before us, a God so majestic and exalted that everything else shrivels up into nothingness in comparison.

Instead of downsizing God, let your imagination go and contemplate His true size. Imagine His filling the whole universe. Picture His reaching out to the farthest stars and even then spilling over into the outermost limits of space. Then kneel before Him and confess that, even so, your vision is still too small.

The universe is big; God is bigger.

Reflections/Prayer Requests

_____

_____

_____

_____

DAY 15

1 Kings 8:33–34

"When Your people Israel are defeated before an enemy because they have sinned against You, and when they turn back to You and confess Your name, and pray and make supplication to You in this temple, then hear in heaven, and forgive the sin of Your people Israel, and bring them back to the land which You gave to their fathers."

No Other Way

In *The Essential Calvin and Hobbes*, by Bill Watterson, the cartoon character Calvin says to his tiger friend, Hobbes, "I feel bad that I called Susie names and hurt her feelings. I'm sorry I did it." "Maybe you should apologize to her," Hobbes suggests. Calvin ponders this for a moment and replies, "I keep hoping there's a less-obvious solution."

We're all like Calvin, aren't we? But sometimes there are no other solutions. The consequences of sin are serious. Wise King Solomon pointed out what Israel eventually would experience as a disobedient nation: defeat and enslavement to her enemies. The Northern Kingdom was taken into captivity in 722 B.C. The Southern Kingdom lasted a little longer, but sin brought about its defeat in 586 B.C. Yet when Israel sincerely confessed her sins before God, as Solomon promised, He restored the people to their land and to Himself.

Sin in a Christian's life also brings defeat. Satan needs only a small foothold in a believer's life, and he will use this advantage to hinder spiritual growth in every possible way. Continued, unconfessed sin ultimately will result in bondage. The only way out is the obvious solution. The apostle John says, "If we confess our sins, He is faithful and just to forgive us our sins and to cleanse us from all unrighteousness" (1 John 1:9).

If you are experiencing spiritual defeat in your life, if you are in bondage to sin, you know what you must do. The solution is obvious. Repent of your sin, confess it to God, agree with Him that in thought, word or deed you have transgressed against Him, and receive His forgiveness. Let the blood of Christ cleanse and restore you.

Don't wait for other solutions; confession of sin is the only way.

Reflections/Prayer Requests

_____

_____

_____

_____

_____

DAY 16

1 Kings 9:4–5

"Now if you walk before Me as your father David walked, in integrity of heart and in uprightness, to do according to all that I have commanded you, and if you keep My statutes and My judgments, then I will establish the throne of your kingdom over Israel forever, as I promised David your father, saying, 'You shall not fail to have a man on the throne of Israel.'"

A Solid Foundation

A very short man wanted to drive a nail in his wall to hang a picture. He stood on a chair, but it wasn't high enough. His wife placed a box on the chair, but he was still too short. Finally she placed a stool on top of the box. Balancing himself precariously, the do-it-yourself picture hanger began to tap timidly with his hammer. "Why don't you hit it hard?" his wife asked. "You'll never drive the nail that way!" Our hero looked down from his perch and replied, "How can a man hit anything hard on a shaky foundation like this?"

Great deeds take solid foundations. God reminded Solomon that if he wanted to establish a great kingdom that would live on through his descendants, he would have to build it on the solid foundation of integrity. Only as Solomon sought to live according to God's commandments and statues would he be assured that future generations of his family would occupy the throne.

Any substitute for integrity is a shaky foundation. We can't build a solid Christian life just on emotional experiences; we have to obey God's Word. We can't raise up a Christian ministry that will endure for decades unless it's done in uprightness of heart. Only integrity is able to provide a solid foundation that God will honor through the ages.

What are you attempting to build today? Is it a family? A ministry? A marriage? A life? Check out your integrity level. Make sure that everything you do is consistent with God's Word. This will not only provide a firm foundation for yourself but will be a blessing to your children as well.

Integrity for the foundation means blessing for the future.

Reflections/Prayer Requests

_____

_____

_____

_____

_____

_____

DAY 17

1 Kings 9:6–7

*"But if you or your sons at all turn from fol-
lowing Me, and do not keep My commandments and My statutes which I have set before you, but go and serve other gods and
worship them, then I will cut off Israel from
the land which I have given them; and this
house which I have consecrated for My name
I will cast out of My sight. Israel will be a
proverb and a byword among all peoples."*

A Symbol of Disaster

In his book *Present Day Parables*, J.
Wilbur Chapman, a late 19th-century evan-
gelist, tells of a town where the name of
Christ was never mentioned except in pro-
fanity. The citizens hung Christ in effigy in
the streets. Then the town was destroyed
by fire. They tried to rebuild, but an Indian
massacre occured. They tried to build
again, and it was partially destroyed by
fire. At last, after much bloodshed and
multiple disasters, the citizens sent to the
American Home Missionary Society and
asked, "Can you send us a minister of
Jesus Christ?" Only after Christ came to
that town did the people have peace and a
degree of prosperity.

God warned Solomon the same would
happen to his kingdom if he or his descendants should ever turn from following
Him. Not only would He remove Israel

from the land, but the consequences would be so dramatic that all the nations around her also would be amazed at what happened. The people would become a symbol of disaster to warn others who might be so foolish.

Israel should be a reminder to every Christian of the dire consequences of leaving God out of our lives. As the descendants of Solomon suffered in the ways God warned them, so believers can experience much pain and loss when they live in disregard to His will and His ways.

Don't forget God. Remember to include Him in the daily routine of your life. Don't just take Him with you to church; take Him to the mall, to the classroom, to the health club. Ask for His guidance in every decision you make, big and little, and look for His hand in every turn of life. When He fills your life, it is full indeed.

We let God down when
we leave Him out.

Reflections/Prayer Requests

_____

_____

_____

_____

_____

_____

DAY 18

1 Kings 10:6–7

*Then she said to the king: "It was a true re-
port which I heard in my own land about your
words and your wisdom. However I did not
believe the words until I came and saw with
my own eyes; and indeed the half was not
told me. Your wisdom and prosperity exceed
the fame of which I heard."*

A Great Day Coming

Since my early school days I had read
about the Grand Canyon. I knew that it
ranges from 4 to 18 miles in width and
more than a mile deep in places. Perhaps
the most impressive part is a 56-mile-long
stretch within the Grand Canyon National
Park. I had even see photos showing the
beautiful colors that stripe the canyon
walls. Yet nothing that I read or saw in a
book prepared me for the awesome experience of standing on the canyon's edge
and seeing for myself the majestic beauty
of this natural wonder.

The Bible says the queen of Sheba had
the same response when she met
Solomon. Sheba was a land hundreds of
miles away in an area now called Yemen,
but this queen had heard stories about Israel's king. The tales told her were suffi-
ciently intriguing to propel her to make
the difficult journey to see Solomon for
herself. Yet when she actually stood in the

presence of Israel's king, she confessed, "The half was not told me."

The same is true for Christians. God's Word speaks of the glorious future that awaits us, yet it also indicates that the half is still to be told. Paul says, "But as it is written: 'Eye has not seen, nor ear heard, nor have entered into the heart of man the things which God has prepared for those who love Him'" (1 Cor. 2:9).

Perhaps you're going through a time of loss and grief right now. Maybe you're feeling lonely and unhappy. Let me encourage you to lift up your head, turn your thoughts away from your present grief and gaze at what God has in store for you. When you stand face-to-face with Jesus, your current distresses will fade away instantly. It will be worth it all when you see Christ.

True reality is not found in today's sorrows but in tomorrow's joys.

Reflections/Prayer Requests

_____

_____

_____

_____

_____

_____

DAY 19

1 Kings 10:23–24

*So King Solomon surpassed all the kings
of the earth in riches and wisdom. And all
the earth sought the presence of Solomon
to hear his wisdom, which God had put
in his heart.*

Seeking God's Wisdom

An American arriving in England for postgraduate study went to visit Nobel Prize-winning poet T. S. Eliot. As the student was leaving, Eliot remarked, "Forty years ago I went from Harvard to Oxford. Now, what advice can I give you?" There was a prolonged pause as the younger man waited breathlessly for the great poet's words of wisdom. Finally Eliot said, "Have you any long underwear?" Good advice for someone going to a cold, damp climate, but hardly the life-shaping wisdom the student hoped for from someone of Eliot's stature.

The poet's visitor may have gone away disappointed, but no one who comes to God for life-changing wisdom ever will go away disillusioned. Solomon, the embodiment of God's wisdom, quickly became a magnet for people all over the known world who were seeking to find meaning in their lives. In a day when travel was both a hardship and extremely dangerous, people nevertheless flocked to hear Solomon speak the wisdom of God.

You can still benefit from Solomon's wisdom. It exists today in such books as Proverbs and Song of Solomon. But Christians have access to much more than the wisdom of the wisest king who ever lived. We have 66 books of wisdom in the Bible, revealed to us through more than 40 Spirit-inspired writers (2 Pet. 1:21). What people in Solomon's day had to travel hundreds of miles to receive, you and I can have simply by opening our Bibles.

Don't neglect the wisdom God has made available to you in Scripture. Find a time every day to read a portion of God's Word. Let the Holy Spirit impart to you practical applications of God's Word to your life. You don't need to cross oceans or climb mountains; just open God's Book.

Wisdom is as near as an open Bible, as distant as a closed one.

Reflections/Prayer Requests

_____

_____

_____

_____

_____

_____

_____

_____

DAY 20

1 Kings 11:1–2

But King Solomon loved many foreign women, as well as the daughter of Pharaoh: women of the Moabites, Ammonites, Edomites, Sidonians, and Hittites—from the nations of whom the LORD had said to the children of Israel, "You shall not intermarry with them, nor they with you. For surely they will turn away your hearts after their gods." Solomon clung to these in love.

Moderation

Good things can become a detriment. In Japan, many golfers carry "hole-in-one" insurance because it is traditional in that culture to share one's good fortune by sending gifts to all your friends when you get an ace. The price for this "albatross," as the Japanese call it, often can reach $10,000. As a result, the good fortune that most golfers would consider a blessing becomes a disaster.

In many ways, marriage is like golf. (Now, stay with me on this!) Marriage is meant by God to be a blessing. God created Eve to be a companion and a helper to Adam (Gen. 2:18). Yet Solomon, by his excesses, turned God's good gift into a disaster. God's ideal has always been one man for one woman, for a lifetime. But that ideal was abused when Solomon gave himself to 700 wives and 300 concubines (1 Kings 11:3). Furthermore, his disobedience to God's command not to marry foreign wives resulted in what God wanted to protect him from—turning his heart toward others gods (v. 4). Intemperance and disobedience became stumbling blocks for this otherwise very wise king.

Christians can fall into the same trap. God has given us many good things: marital intimacy, food, pleasure, sleep. But practiced to extremes, such good gifts can become the sins of lust, gluttony, licentiousness and sloth. Satan loves to take what is wholesome and blessed from God and make it a snare to the unwary. That is why Paul says, "Everyone who competes for the prize is temperate in all things" (1 Cor. 9:25).

Take care that you keep all things in balance. Even though it may be a good gift from God, it can cause you to stumble if practiced without moderation. Enjoy God's gifts, but practice temperance in everything you enjoy.

If practiced in excess, even good things can become bad.

Reflections/Prayer Requests

DAY 21

1 Kings 11:11–12

Therefore the LORD said to Solomon, "Because you have done this, and have not kept My covenant and My statutes, which I have commanded you, I will surely tear the kingdom away from you and give it to your servant. Nevertheless I will not do it in your days, for the sake of your father David; but I will tear it out of the hand of your son."

Judgment With Mercy

A young employee misappropriated several hundred dollars. When his theft was discovered he was told to report to the office of the firm's senior partner. The young man knew he would lose his job and possibly face legal action. When he was questioned he admitted his guilt. Then, surprisingly, he was asked, "If I keep you in your present job, can I trust you in the future?" The young worker brightened, "Yes, sir, you surely can." The executive responded, "I'm not going to press charges, and you can continue in your present responsibility." He concluded, "I think you ought to know, however, that you are the second man in this firm who succumbed to temptation and was shown leniency. I was the first. The mercy you are receiving, I received. It is only the grace of God that can keep us both."

Solomon was like that employee. He also was guilty of sin. His foreign wives

44

turned his heart toward other gods. Yet as God confronted this once-faithful king, He showed mercy. He delayed the removal of the kingdom from Solomon until the days of his son Rehoboam, and even then God promised to leave one tribe, Judah, for Solomon's son to rule.

People will commit sins against us—sometimes grievous sins. Occasionally, those sins require consequences. Yet as we carry out judgment, let's not forget to be merciful. After all, God didn't forget mercy when He was dealing with us.

When the need arises, pray that God will not only give you wisdom in meting out to others the consequences of their sin but also give you the grace to show mercy. When judgment becomes necessary, mercy becomes momentous.

If godly justice didn't involve gracious mercy, we all would be doomed.

Reflections/Prayer Requests

DAY 22

1 Kings 11:14, 23

Now the LORD raised up an adversary against Solomon, Hadad the Edomite; he was a descendant of the king in Edom.

And God raised up another adversary against him, Rezon the son of Eliadah, who had fled from his lord, Hadadezer king of Zobah.

Blessed Adversary

In his book *Pain: The Tool of the Wounded Surgeon*, Philip Yancey reminds us that pain can serve a definite purpose in our lives. He cites Dr. Paul Brand, one of the world's foremost experts on leprosy, who worked on the mission field with lepers for years. Dr. Brand observed that "leprosy patients lose their fingers and toes, not because the disease causes decay, but precisely because they lack pain sensations. Nothing warns them when water is too hot or a hammer handle is splintered. Accidental self-abuse destroys their bodies." They need pain to alert them to danger.

God uses distressing situations much the same way. Solomon needed to be alerted to his headlong rush into sin, so God used pain. To inflict that pain, God raised up adversaries who would harass and torment this sin-numbed king until he would turn and repent. God did not plague

Solomon in order to punish him but to keep him from the destruction of sin.

The Lord uses this same approach with us today. When one of His children becomes desensitized to sin, God allows painful circumstances to intervene sometimes by way of an adversary. The writer of Hebrews says, "Now no chastening seems to be joyful for the present, but grievous; nevertheless, afterward it yields the peaceable fruit of righteousness to those who have been trained by it" (12:11). Adversaries can be the hand of God's blessing in disguise.

If you have an adversary, treat him or her as a God-given gift. Ask the Lord to reveal to you what issues He would have you be aware of through the chastising ministry of this individual. Take heed to your adversary, and let God protect you from self-destruction. See your adversary as God's means of sensitizing you to danger and defeat.

A good adversary is as valuable as a good friend.

Reflections/Prayer Requests

_____

_____

_____

_____

DAY 23

And he said to Jeroboam, "Take for yourself ten pieces, for thus says the LORD, the God of Israel: 'Behold, I will tear the kingdom out of the hand of Solomon and will give ten tribes to you (but he shall have one tribe for the sake of My servant David, and for the sake of Jerusalem, the city which I have chosen out of all the tribes of Israel).'"

The Tragedy of Division

The pastor of a small church was on his way home when he met an acquaintance from town. After chatting a while the man asked how many members he had. The pastor responded, "Fifty active members." The friend said, "My, that certainly speaks well for you." The preacher responded, "Well, I wouldn't say that. All fifty are active—but twenty-five are actively working for me and the other twenty-five are actively working against me!"

Solomon's son Rehoboam had even worse odds. Of the 12 tribes that originally made up the nation of Israel, only 2, Judah and Benjamin, would remain loyal to the house of David. The other 10 would desert him in favor of a leader more to their liking. As history proved, however, this was a mistake. By turning against the lineage of David, God's chosen one, Israel became ensnared in idolatry and was eventually destroyed in 722 B.C. by the Assyrians.

48

Division within the Body of Christ is never a good thing. Seldom does it lead to anything beneficial for those involved. People are always hurt and the testimony of the church is tarnished. The apostle Paul said, "For where there are envy, strife, and divisions among you, are you not carnal and behaving like mere men?" (1 Cor. 3:3). Instead, he advised, "Be at peace among yourselves" (1 Thess. 5:13).

If you are part of a divided church, what might you do to bring about healing and unity? Whom should you go to? Whom should you talk to? What can God and you do together? Ask Him to give you the wisdom to be a peacemaker. Don't be a part of the problem; be a part of the solution.

Dividing a church is like killing half your body; it always destroys the other half too.

Reflections/Prayer Requests

_____

_____

_____

_____

_____

_____

_____

_____

DAY 24

1 Kings 11:36

"And to his son I will give one tribe, that My servant David may always have a lamp before Me in Jerusalem, the city which I have chosen for Myself, to put My name there."

A Special Place

My responsibilities in ministry require that I travel a lot, so I have been to many beautiful and exotic places. But there's one place that's extra special. No matter where I go, this place is not far from my heart or mind—it's called home. No other place can match it. Where else can I enjoy my family, visit with my friends and just put my feet up and relax? That's what makes it so special.

God also has a special place—it's called Jerusalem. David conquered this city, originally occupied by the Jebusites, soon after he was anointed king over all of Israel (2 Sam. 5:1–10). Here, David built his palace and governed the nation. And here, Solomon built God's house. The Ark of the Covenant (the symbol of God's presence) was placed in the Holy of Holies, and thousands flocked to worship God in His holy temple. And through all the centuries since, Jerusalem has remained a special city to Jews, Christians, Muslims and, most of all, to God, who chose to put His name there.

When Christ died on the cross, however, God established another special place—not of stone and mortar, but the heart of anyone who believes in Him. What was promised in the Old Testament (Ezek. 11:19-20) was fulfilled through Christ (1 Cor. 3:16). God has literally placed His name upon us, and we are called "Christians."

Have you made your heart a special place to God? You can, by inviting Jesus Christ to be your Savior. Sincerely surrender your life to Him, accept His forgiveness for your sins, and let Him put His name upon you. The Lord has set aside a special people, and you can be one of them.

God has a special place in the heart of His special people.

Reflections/Prayer Requests

_____

_____

_____

_____

_____

_____

_____

_____

DAY 25

1 Kings 11:40-41

Solomon therefore sought to kill Jeroboam. But Jeroboam arose and fled to Egypt, to Shishak king of Egypt, and was in Egypt until the death of Solomon. Now the rest of the acts of Solomon, all that he did, and his wisdom, are they not written in the book of the acts of Solomon?

Your Reactions Are Showing

In his book *The Message in Your Emotions*, Wayne McDill reflects, "Emotions cloud our normal thinking processes and often cause us to react in ways we shouldn't. We say things in anger that hurt the ones we love most. We buy a new car in the excitement of its appeal. We cry and lose our composure, adding embarrassment to insecurity. We laugh when it really isn't funny because we are uncomfortable." It's little wonder that a long time ago Plato wrote, "The passionate are like men standing on their heads; they see all things the wrong way."

Solomon was a passionate man who allowed his emotions to cause him to react in the wrong way. When God raised up Jeroboam to chastise Solomon for his sins, instead of repenting, the king attempted to have the young man killed. Solomon allowed his emotions to obscure his wisdom, and the consequences were tragic. At Solomon's death, Jeroboam returned from exile and seized control of the ten northern tribes. He became a thorn in the side to Rehoboam, who succeeded his father as king in Judah.

When God brings chastisement into our lives, we, like Solomon, often react emotionally rather than wisely. Instead of allowing God's discipline to bring us to repentance, we seek for ways to avoid the consequences. We run the wrong direction. We become defensive of our behavior. We look for ways to excuse our actions. We grow bitter rather than better. We see everything the wrong way.

Let God's discipline do its work in your life. Instead of allowing your emotions to rule your reactions, respond with a wisdom that allows you to benefit from this experience. Discover what God wants to do in your life, and let Him do it.

Right reaction is the father of righteous behavior.

Reflections/Prayer Requests

_____

_____

_____

_____

_____

DAY 26

2 Chronicles 2:4–5

Behold, I am building a temple for the name of the LORD my God, to dedicate it to Him, to burn before Him sweet incense, for the continual showbread, for the burnt offerings morning and evening, on the Sabbaths, on the New Moons, and on the set feasts of the LORD our God. This is an ordinance forever to Israel. And the temple which I build will be great, for our God is greater than all gods.

The Greatest of All

In 1934 the Cunard ship-building company was getting ready to name its greatest ocean liner, a vessel more than 1,000 feet long and capable of crossing the Atlantic in just over four days. The consensus of opinion was that it should be named after Queen Elizabeth I. A high official reportedly went to King George V and announced, "We would like to name the ship after England's greatest queen." "Well," said the king, "I shall have to ask her." Consequently the ship was promptly named after his wife, Queen Mary!

If we're not specific when we speak, a lot of confusion can result. No such confusion, however, existed in Solomon's mind when it came to honoring God. He was intent upon building a great temple because "our God is greater than all gods." A multitude of gods existed in the nations around Israel—Baal, Molech and Asherah, for example. These, however, were only demonic spirits (1 Cor. 10:19-20) or statues of stone. Solomon knew there was only One who was truly God.

Too often we forget that our God is greater than all other powers, human or supernatural. We needn't fear any foe. The psalmist said, "A thousand may fall at your side, and ten thousand at your right hand; but it shall not come near you" (Ps. 91:7). God's hand of protection is upon us until He chooses to call us home, and none can challenge His authority. No god is greater than our God.

Take courage. Rest completely in the God who is above all gods. He is your strength and protection. He will keep you when all others fail. He is the greatest of all.

Since God has no equal, He has no challenger.

Reflections/Prayer Requests

_____

_____

_____

_____

_____

_____

DAY 27

2 Chronicles 6:10

"So the LORD has fulfilled His word which He spoke, and I have filled the position of my father David, and sit on the throne of Israel, as the LORD promised; and I have built the temple for the name of the LORD God of Israel."

The Promise Maker

Clarence McCartney, a pastor during the first half of the 20th century, used to tell the story of a man who appeared daily outside the Brooklyn city hall. He had been a man of some influence in the city. In a time of financial difficulty, however, a friend promised to meet him there at noon and loan him a large sum of money. But the friend did not keep his promise. Disappointment broke the man's heart and skewed his mind. Every day after that, he would come and look wistfully at the clock, waiting for it to strike twelve, looking in vain for the friend who promised he would come but never did.

How different this situation is from the relationship that Solomon experienced with God. Jehovah is the God who "fulfilled His word" to Solomon's father, David, and to Solomon himself. All that the Lord had promised He performed. He had kept David safe through years of warfare, brought his son Solomon to the throne and then helped Solomon build a magnificent temple to show His glory. Everything that the Lord said to David and Solomon came true just as He had promised.

God has not changed (Heb. 13:8). He is still keeping His promises; they are as dependable as ever. When God speaks through His Word, you can be sure that what He says will come to pass. When He declares, "I will never leave you" (Heb. 13:5), "I will guide you" (Ps. 32:8), "My grace is sufficient for you" (2 Cor. 12:9), and I "shall supply all your need" (Phil. 4:19), He means it. He will never fail us. He will never go back on His word.

Take your stand on God's promises. You will never be on a more solid footing. Trust Him. If God has said it, He will do it.

***The promises God makes
He never breaks.***

Reflections/Prayer Requests

_____

_____

_____

_____

_____

_____

_____

DAY 28

2 Chronicles 7:14

*"If My people who are called by My name will
humble themselves, and pray and seek My
face, and turn from their wicked ways, then I
will hear from heaven, and will forgive their sin
and heal their land."*

Prescription for Revival

Richard Owen Roberts observed,
"There is a sense in which revival is like a
prairie fire ignited by a bolt of lightning
from the heavens. Without organization,
advertising or even sometimes human
leadership, revivals have altered the
hearts of men, the social attitudes of millions and the destinies of nations." Revival
is the heartfelt prayer of many of us, and
God's Word gives the only prescription for
revival. We don't just have to wait pas-
sively; we can actively be a part of the
process.

When Solomon concluded the dedica-
tion of the temple, the Lord appeared to
him. The king knew that his people would
be pulled away from the Lord at various
times, and he wanted some assurance
that God would not give up on them. In
answer to his prayers, God assured
Solomon that even in times when He
would bring hard judgment on Israel because of her sin, revival would still be possible, but it must begin with God's people.

Furthermore, His people must meet certain requirements. Only then would God forgive and restore.

The same is true today. Instead of the nation of Israel, however, it is now the church that needs revived. Yet the standards are still the same. First we need a spirit of humility. Pride will block any attempt at revival. Then we must commit to praying and seeking God's face. Our priorities must change to put an emphasis on communicating with God in both confession and fellowship. But the prescription is not complete until we turn from our sins. When we're willing to change our behavior as well as our attitude, God promises to cleanse and renew us.

If you know Christ as your Savior, apply the steps from this verse to your life. Humbly seek the Lord in prayer; put away your sins and experience a new beginning with God. You don't have to wait for a national revival to experience personal revival.

Revival has to begin with someone; let it be you.

Reflections/Prayer Requests

_____

_____

_____

_____

DAY 29

*Yes, if you cry out for discernment, and lift up
your voice for understanding, if you seek her
as silver, and search for her as for hidden
treasures; then you will understand the fear of
the LORD, and find the knowledge of God.*

Searching God

One of the better-known treasure
hunts of modern times is the quest to find
the rumored wealth known as the "Beale
treasure." The hunt began when an ec-
centric man who left the East for the gold
and silver mines of the West returned
home, supposedly hid a vast amount of
wealth and then disappeared forever. All
he left behind were several messages
written in a mysterious code. When deci-
phered, one of those messages told of the
treasure and its approximate location. The
other documents, which no one has been
able to interpret, supposedly pinpoint the
site. Since the Beale documents first came
to light, thousands of man-hours and hundreds of thousands of dollars have been
spent attempting to break the codes and
find the legendary treasure.

Solomon noted, however, that if we put
the same amount of time and effort into a
relationship with God as we do into
searching for earthly treasure, we will find
a fortune that is far greater. The reward

for our efforts will not be silver or gold but an intimacy with God that is far more meaningful. Speaking as one of the richest men who ever lived, Solomon knew that living in the presence of an awesome God is the greatest treasure that can be found.

There is nothing wrong with material treasures. Abraham, Job, David and Solomon were all blessed with great wealth. But the focus of their lives was not on gaining possessions; it was on knowing God. Today, Christians face the same challenge. In a materialistic world that urges us to gather and hoard an abundance of things, what we really need is a closer relationship with God. That's the real treasure.

Make sure that you aren't cheated by earthly treasure. Put as much effort into drawing closer to God as you do in collecting possessions. Let your life be filled with His awesomeness, and you'll never want for wealth.

Seeking God always yields treasure.

Reflections/Prayer Requests

_____

_____

_____

_____

_____

DAY 30

*Trust in the LORD with all your heart,
and lean not on your own understanding;
in all your ways acknowledge Him,
and He shall direct your paths.*

Trust in the Lord

Everyone should know that human wisdom is very fallible. In spite of that, a woman in Haifa, Israel, is suing a television weatherman in small claims court for $1,000 after he predicted sunshine for a day that turned out to be stormy. The woman claims the forecast caused her to leave home lightly dressed. As a result, she caught the flu, missed four days' work, spent $38 on medication and suffered stress. Whether the legal system agrees with her or not, however, it's obvious that she reaped the consequences of trusting in human wisdom.

Solomon believed that no one should rely upon his own understanding. Instead, he declared, place your trust in God and seek His wisdom in every aspect of life. The promise God gave through this wise king is that, in return, He will direct your steps into the right path. God never makes a wrong prediction.

Most things, including the weather, are understood very imperfectly even by people who have spent many years studying them. At best, we can only make educated guesses. If those guesses prove true, it's still usually beyond our control to change our circumstances. The Lord, on the other hand, possesses all knowledge (Ps. 139:4-6). Furthermore, He is in control of all things—not only the weather (Mark 4:39), but illnesses (Matt. 8:3; Mark 1:30-34) and death itself (John 11:43-44). Every nation of the earth is at His mercy (Ps. 2:1-9). What He declares will come to pass. You can count on it.

In the Bible you'll find the wisdom of God. Trust Him to guide you when you read His Word. Be confident that He will direct your paths as you apply the Scriptures to your life. Take every opportunity, every difficulty, every issue that comes up in your life and let God show you His way through His Word.

When you read God's Word you read God's mind.

Reflections/Prayer Requests

_____

_____

_____

_____

_____

_____

_____

DAY 31

Proverbs 8:35–36

"For whoever finds me finds life, and obtains favor from the LORD; but he who sins against me wrongs his own soul; all those who hate me love death."

Finding Life

Many people, especially in the field of astronomy, are eagerly seeking signs of life in outer space. A couple of years ago, NASA scientists shook the world by announcing that they had found evidence—embedded in a meteor that had fallen to earth—that primitive life once existed on the planet Mars. After all the hoopla died down, these findings were called into question. Others who have studied the data sent back by the *Galileo* space probe are suggesting the possibility of life on one of Jupiter's moons. However flimsy the straw, scientists seem ready to grasp it as long as it points to the possibility of life on other planets.

While the possibility of finding life in outer space is intriguing, we don't need to look there to find life. Real life is found in the Lord Jesus Christ, who came to earth so we could know Him. God promises that anyone who comes to know Jesus in a saving way finds real life—a life of quality as well as quantity, a life that will experience the joy of being in His presence forever (Rev. 22:3–5).

Many people today are looking for life. If they aren't looking for it on other planets, they are searching for something special on this planet. They seek it in their pleasures and search for it in unfulfilling relationships. Quietly, but desperately, they hunt for something that will make their life worthwhile. Yet all the time God stands ready to provide the very thing they're lacking—a life that has meaning for today as well as eternity. All they have to do is receive Christ as their Savior.

If you are looking for life, look to the Lord. The apostle John wrote, "He who has the Son has life; he who does not have the Son of God does not have life" (1 John 5:12). You don't have to be a scientist to find life. You just have to know where to look.

Life is found through a relationship with Christ, not a telescope.

Reflections/Prayer Requests

_____

_____

_____

_____

_____

_____

_____

GIANTS OF THE OLD TESTAMENT

Look for these other titles
in the series:

Also coming in 1999: